# Raising Confident Kids In Recreative Parenting

## *Simple and revolutionary strategies to promote your child's developing intelligence*

Charles Baskin

# Contents

# Introduction



## *Why Recreative Parenting?*

Parenting in the modern world requires a dynamic approach that adapts to the changing needs of children and the evolving societal landscape. Traditional parenting methods, while foundational, often fall short in addressing the nuanced challenges faced by today's families. Recreative parenting, a term that encapsulates creativity, responsiveness, and adaptability, emerges as a revolutionary approach to child-rearing that prioritizes the holistic development of children.

Recreative parenting is not about following a rigid set of rules. Instead, it embraces flexibility and innovation, allowing parents to tailor their methods to the unique needs and personalities of their children. This approach recognizes that every child is different and that parenting strategies must evolve to foster a child's individual strengths and interests. It also underscores the importance of fostering a nurturing environment where children feel safe to explore, make mistakes, and learn from their experiences.

One of the core principles of recreative parenting is the emphasis on play and creativity as vital components of learning. Play is not merely a leisure activity but a fundamental way through which children understand the world around them. By integrating play into everyday learning, parents can enhance their children's cognitive, emotional, and social skills. Recreative parenting also promotes active engagement, where parents participate alongside their children in creative activities, thereby strengthening the parent-child bond and encouraging mutual respect and understanding.

Furthermore, recreative parenting acknowledges the role of emotional intelligence and empathy in child development. It encourages parents to model empathetic behavior, helping children to develop strong emotional regulation skills and a deep sense of compassion. This approach not only nurtures emotional well-being but also equips children with the tools to build healthy relationships and navigate social complexities.

In essence, recreative parenting is about being proactive and present, continuously adapting strategies to meet the developmental needs of children. It is a holistic approach that integrates creativity, empathy, and play into the fabric of everyday life, ensuring that children grow up confident, capable, and emotionally resilient.

## *The Importance of Confidence in Child Development*

Confidence is the cornerstone of a child's development, influencing their academic performance, social interactions, and overall well-being. Confident children are more likely to take on challenges, persevere in the face of difficulties, and develop a positive self-image. Conversely, a lack of confidence can hinder a child's ability to explore new opportunities and can lead to feelings of inadequacy and anxiety.

The importance of confidence in child development cannot be overstated. It affects every aspect of a child's life, from their ability to form friendships to their capacity to handle stress. Confidence is built through a combination of factors, including parental support, positive reinforcement, and the opportunities children are given to succeed and fail in a safe environment.

One of the key elements in building confidence is fostering a sense of self-worth. Children need to feel valued and loved for who they are, not just for their achievements. This sense of unconditional acceptance from parents provides a solid foundation upon which children can build their self-esteem. Encouraging children to express themselves, listen to their opinions, and validate their feelings are critical steps in this process.

Another important factor is resilience. Confident children are resilient; they view challenges as opportunities to grow rather than as insurmountable obstacles. Parents can help build resilience by teaching problem-solving skills and encouraging a growth mindset, where effort and perseverance are valued over inherent talent. This helps children understand that failure is a part of learning and not a reflection of their worth.

Social competence also plays a significant role in the development of confidence. Children who are confident in their social skills are better equipped to navigate the complexities of peer relationships. Parents can support this by modeling positive social interactions and providing opportunities for children to practice these skills in a variety of settings.

Overall, confidence is essential for a child's healthy development. It empowers children to explore their potential, engage with the world around them, and develop into well-rounded individuals. By fostering confidence, parents set their children on a path to success and fulfillment.

## How to Use This Book

"Raising Confident Kids in Recreative Parenting" is designed to be a practical guide for parents who want to embrace a more dynamic and responsive approach to child-rearing. The book is structured to provide both theoretical insights and actionable strategies that can be easily integrated into daily routines. Here's how you can make the most out of this book:

**1. Start with Self-Reflection:** Before diving into the chapters, take some time to reflect on your current parenting style. What are your strengths? What areas do you feel need improvement? This self-awareness will help you tailor the strategies in this book to fit your unique situation.

**2. Read Sequentially or Selectively:** The book is organized into chapters that build upon each other, but each chapter can also stand alone. If you're facing specific challenges, feel free to jump directly to the relevant section. However, reading the book sequentially will provide a comprehensive understanding of recreative parenting.

**3. Engage with Activities and Worksheets:** Throughout the book, you'll find activities and worksheets designed to reinforce the concepts discussed. These are not mere add-ons but integral parts of the learning process. Engaging with these materials will help you apply the strategies in a practical context.

**_4. Reflect and Adapt:_** At the end of each chapter, there are reflection questions and prompts. Use these to think about how the concepts apply to your own parenting journey. Parenting is not one-size-fits-all, and these reflections will help you adapt the strategies to suit your family's needs.

**_5. Implement Gradually:_** Change can be overwhelming, so take it one step at a time. Implement the strategies gradually, allowing yourself and your children time to adjust. Celebrate small victories along the way and be patient with setbacks.

**_6. Join a Community:_** Parenting can sometimes feel isolating, but remember, you're not alone. Consider joining parenting groups or online forums where you can share experiences, seek advice, and find support from other parents on the same journey.

**_7. Revisit and Revise:_** As your children grow and your family dynamics change, revisit the book to reassess and revise your strategies. Recreative parenting is an ongoing process, and continuous learning and adaptation are key to its success.

By using this book as a guide and resource, you'll be equipped to foster a deep sense of self-worth, encourage creativity and problem-solving skills, develop emotional intelligence, and build a strong, loving relationship with your child. The journey to raising confident kids is a continuous one, and this book is here to support you every step of the way.

# Chapter 1: Building Self-Worth & Self-Acceptance

## *1.1 Understanding Self-Worth*

Self-worth is a fundamental aspect of a child's development, influencing their emotional health, academic performance, and social interactions. Understanding self-worth involves recognizing it as an intrinsic value that a person places on themselves, independent of external achievements or validations. It is about feeling inherently worthy and valuable simply for who they are.

Self-worth differs from self-esteem, though the two are often used interchangeably. Self-esteem is generally more related to how a child feels about their abilities and achievements. In contrast, self-worth is a deeper, more stable sense of being valuable regardless of circumstances. For children, developing a strong sense of self-worth can protect against the negative effects of criticism and failure, providing a buffer against the challenges they will inevitably face.

The foundations of self-worth are laid early in life. Babies and toddlers form their initial self-worth based on the responsiveness and affection of their caregivers. When parents consistently meet their needs and provide a loving, secure environment, children learn that they are valued and worthy of care. This early foundation is crucial, as it sets the stage for how children perceive themselves throughout their lives.

As children grow, their sense of self-worth continues to develop through their interactions with family, friends, and teachers. Positive experiences, such as being listened to, respected, and encouraged, reinforce their sense of worth. Negative experiences, such as criticism, neglect, or bullying, can undermine it. Therefore, parents play a critical role in helping their children build and maintain a healthy sense of self-worth.

Encouraging self-worth involves several key practices:

- **Unconditional Love and Acceptance:** Show children that they are loved and valued for who they are, not just for what they achieve.
- **Validation of Feelings:** Acknowledge and validate children's emotions, helping them understand that their feelings are important and legitimate.
- **Encouraging Autonomy:** Allow children to make choices and take responsibility for their actions, fostering a sense of control and competence.
- **Providing Positive Role Models:** Model self-worth through your behavior. Show self-compassion and self-respect, demonstrating how to value oneself.

A strong sense of self-worth is essential for children to develop resilience and a positive self-image. It helps them navigate challenges, build healthy relationships, and approach life with confidence and optimism.

## 1.2 Strategies for Nurturing Self-Acceptance

Self-acceptance is a crucial aspect of self-worth, involving the recognition and acceptance of all facets of oneself, including strengths and weaknesses. It means understanding that one's value is not diminished by imperfections or failures. For children, nurturing self-acceptance involves helping them recognize and embrace their unique qualities.

Here are several strategies for fostering self-acceptance in children:

## Promote a Growth Mindset:

- Encourage Effort Over Outcomes: Praise children for their efforts and perseverance rather than solely for their achievements. This helps them see value in their hard work and understand that failure is a part of learning.
- Model Resilience: Show how to handle setbacks positively. Discuss your own challenges and how you overcame them, demonstrating that everyone makes mistakes and that these do not define their worth.

## Create a Safe and Supportive Environment:

- Encourage Open Communication: Foster an environment where children feel safe to express their thoughts and feelings without fear of judgment or criticism.
- Provide Consistent Support: Be a reliable source of encouragement and support. Consistency in your responses helps children feel secure and valued.

## Celebrate Individuality:

- Recognize Unique Strengths: Help children identify and celebrate their unique strengths and interests. This boosts their confidence and helps them appreciate their individuality.
- Respect Differences: Teach children to value diversity and respect differences in others, which in turn helps them accept their own uniqueness.

## Teach Self-Compassion:

- Encourage Kindness to Oneself: Teach children to treat themselves with the same kindness and understanding they would offer a friend. This involves recognizing their own struggles without harsh self-criticism.

- Practice Mindfulness: Introduce mindfulness practices that help children stay grounded and present, reducing anxiety about past mistakes or future challenges.

## Set Realistic Expectations:

- Avoid Perfectionism: Help children understand that perfection is not a realistic or necessary goal. Emphasize progress and learning over flawless performance.
- Set Achievable Goals: Work with children to set realistic, attainable goals. Celebrate their progress, no matter how small, to reinforce their sense of accomplishment.

## Encourage Reflection:

- Journaling: Encourage children to keep a journal where they can reflect on their experiences, emotions, and growth. This practice helps them gain perspective and appreciate their progress.

- Discussion: Regularly discuss their experiences and feelings, helping them process and understand their journey towards self-acceptance.

Nurturing self-acceptance in children involves a consistent and compassionate approach. By creating a supportive environment, promoting a growth mindset, and encouraging individuality, parents can help their children develop a healthy and resilient sense of self.

## 1.3 Positive Reinforcement Techniques

Positive reinforcement is a powerful tool in promoting desired behaviors and boosting a child's self-worth. It involves providing rewards or positive outcomes following a behavior, thereby increasing the likelihood that the behavior will be repeated. When used effectively, positive reinforcement can foster a positive, supportive environment where children feel valued and motivated.

Here are some effective positive reinforcement techniques:

## *Verbal Praise:*

- Specific Praise: Instead of general comments like "Good job," provide specific feedback that acknowledges the effort or behavior, such as "I'm really proud of how you cleaned your room without being asked."
- Sincerity: Ensure that praise is genuine and heartfelt. Children can usually tell when praise is insincere, which can undermine its effectiveness.

## *Tangible Rewards:*

- Reward Systems: Implement reward systems like sticker charts or point systems that can be exchanged for privileges or small prizes. This helps children see a tangible connection between their actions and positive outcomes.
- Occasional Surprises: Sometimes surprise rewards can be very effective. A spontaneous

treat or extra playtime for good behavior can reinforce positive actions.

## *Privileges and Opportunities:*

- Extra Privileges: Granting extra privileges, such as additional screen time or a later bedtime, can be a powerful motivator.
- Special Activities: Allow children to choose a special activity as a reward for positive behavior, like a family outing or a favorite meal.

## *Positive Attention:*

- Quality Time: Spend quality time with your child as a form of reinforcement. This could be playing a game together, reading a book, or simply talking. The attention and time you give can be a powerful reward.
- Public Acknowledgment: Recognize their achievements in front of others, such as family members or peers. This not only reinforces the behavior but also boosts their self-esteem.

## *Encouragement and Support:*

- Encouraging Effort: Regularly encourage children's efforts and progress, not just their successes. This helps them understand that effort and persistence are valued.
- Constructive Feedback: When providing feedback, focus on the positive aspects and offer constructive suggestions for improvement. This helps maintain their motivation and confidence.

## *Consistency and Fairness:*

- Consistency: Be consistent in your use of positive reinforcement. Inconsistent reinforcement can confuse children and reduce the effectiveness of this technique.
- Fairness: Ensure that rewards are appropriate and fair. Avoid favoritism or unfair distribution of rewards, as this can create resentment and reduce the effectiveness of positive reinforcement.

Positive reinforcement is most effective when it is used in conjunction with clear expectations and consistent boundaries. Here are some additional tips for implementing positive reinforcement:

- Set Clear Expectations: Clearly communicate the behaviors you expect and the rewards that will follow. Children need to understand what is expected of them and what they can earn through positive actions.
- Be Immediate: Try to provide reinforcement as soon as possible after the desired behavior. This helps children make a clear connection between their actions and the positive outcome.
- Vary the Reinforcements: Use a variety of reinforcements to keep children motivated. Mixing verbal praise with tangible rewards and special privileges can prevent the reinforcement from becoming predictable and losing its effectiveness.
- Monitor and Adjust: Regularly monitor the effectiveness of your reinforcement techniques and adjust as needed. What works for one child or situation may not work for another, so be flexible and willing to try different approaches.

Positive reinforcement, when used effectively, can significantly enhance a child's self-worth and motivation. By recognizing and rewarding desired behaviors, parents can create a supportive environment that fosters confidence, resilience, and a positive self-image.

## 1.4 The Role of Unconditional Love

Unconditional love is a cornerstone of healthy child development, forming the bedrock upon which a child's sense of self-worth and security is built. It is the type of love that is given freely without conditions or expectations. This love remains constant regardless of the child's behavior, achievements, or failures, and it communicates to the child that they are valued for who they are, not for what they do.

The impact of unconditional love on a child's emotional and psychological well-being is profound. When children know they are loved unconditionally, they develop a secure attachment to their parents or caregivers. This secure attachment is crucial as it provides a safe base from which children can explore the world, take risks, and develop independence. They are more likely to engage confidently in new experiences and learn from their mistakes because they know their value is not contingent on their success or failure.

Unconditional love also promotes resilience. Children who feel loved unconditionally are better equipped to handle stress and adversity. They understand that setbacks and challenges do not diminish their worth. This resilience is vital for navigating the ups and downs of life, fostering a positive outlook and a willingness to persevere through difficulties.

A key aspect of unconditional love is acceptance. This means accepting children for who they are, including their unique personalities, interests, and quirks. It involves appreciating their individuality and encouraging them to embrace their authentic selves. When children feel accepted, they are more likely to develop self-acceptance, which is crucial for building self-esteem and confidence. They learn to value their strengths and acknowledge their weaknesses without shame or fear of rejection.

Unconditional love also involves being present and attentive. Quality time spent together, active listening, and showing genuine interest in their thoughts and feelings convey that they are important and valued. This presence reinforces the child's sense of security and belonging. Moreover, it helps build a strong parent-child bond, which is essential for healthy emotional and social development.

Discipline, too, plays a role in unconditional love. It might seem contradictory, but setting boundaries and enforcing rules is a form of love. Consistent, fair discipline helps children understand limits and develop self-control. However, it is crucial that discipline is administered in a manner that separates the behavior from the child's worth. For example, instead of saying "You are a bad child," it is more effective to say, "The behavior you exhibited was not acceptable." This approach ensures that the child understands that while their behavior may be subject to consequences, their inherent value remains intact.

One of the most powerful ways to demonstrate unconditional love is through physical affection. Hugs, kisses, and other forms of physical closeness provide comfort and security. Physical affection is a non-verbal way of expressing love and can be particularly effective in soothing children during times of stress or anxiety.

Moreover, unconditional love is about being patient and forgiving. Children are bound to make mistakes as they learn and grow. Responding to their mistakes with patience and forgiveness teaches them that it is okay to be imperfect and that they are still loved despite their flaws. This approach helps children develop a healthy attitude toward failure, viewing it as an opportunity for growth rather than a source of shame.

Unconditional love also means being a role model. Children learn a great deal from observing their parents' behavior. By modeling self-love, compassion, and empathy, parents can teach their children to treat themselves and others with kindness and respect. This modeling helps children internalize these values and apply them in their own lives.

Ultimately, the role of unconditional love in a child's life cannot be overstated. It provides the foundation for emotional security, self-worth, and resilience. It fosters an environment where children feel safe to be themselves, take risks, and learn from their experiences. By consistently showing unconditional love, parents can help their children develop into confident, well-adjusted individuals capable of forming healthy relationships and leading fulfilling lives.

## 1.5 Overcoming Negative Self-Talk

Negative self-talk can significantly undermine a child's self-esteem and overall well-being. It refers to the internal dialogue that reflects negative thoughts and beliefs about oneself. This type of self-talk can become deeply ingrained and influence how children perceive themselves and their abilities. Overcoming negative self-talk is crucial for fostering a positive self-image and building resilience.

Negative self-talk often stems from various sources, including critical feedback from others, comparisons with peers, and unrealistic standards set by society or even the children themselves. These negative messages can become internalized, leading children to doubt their worth and abilities. It is essential to address and challenge these negative thoughts to prevent them from taking root and causing long-term harm.

One of the first steps in overcoming negative self-talk is to help children become aware of their internal dialogue. Many children might not even realize they are engaging in negative self-talk. Encouraging them to articulate their thoughts and feelings can help bring these negative patterns to light. This awareness is the first step toward change, as it allows children to recognize when they are being self-critical.

Once children are aware of their negative self-talk, it is important to teach them to challenge these thoughts. This involves questioning the validity of the negative messages they tell themselves. For example, if a child thinks, "I am terrible at math," they can be encouraged to reflect on instances where they performed well or made progress in math. This process helps them see that their negative thoughts are often exaggerated and not reflective of reality.

Replacing negative self-talk with positive affirmations is another effective strategy. Positive affirmations are constructive statements that can help reframe a child's mindset. Encouraging children to create and repeat affirmations such as "I am capable," "I can improve with practice," or "I am worthy" can gradually shift their internal dialogue from negative to positive. It is important that these affirmations are realistic and achievable, as overly grandiose statements might feel insincere and be dismissed by the child.

Another important aspect of overcoming negative self-talk is fostering a growth mindset. A growth mindset is the belief that abilities and intelligence can be developed through effort and learning. This contrasts with a fixed mindset, which holds that abilities are static and unchangeable. By encouraging a growth mindset, parents can help children see challenges and failures as opportunities for growth rather than as reflections of their worth. This perspective reduces the likelihood of negative self-talk, as children become more focused on learning and improvement rather than judging themselves harshly.

Parents play a crucial role in modeling positive self-talk and a growth mindset. Children often mimic the behaviors and attitudes of their parents. By demonstrating self-compassion, acknowledging personal mistakes without harsh self-criticism, and viewing challenges as learning opportunities, parents can show their children how to engage in positive self-talk. This modeling can be incredibly influential in shaping a child's internal dialogue.

Providing a supportive and encouraging environment is also essential. When children feel supported and valued by their parents and caregivers, they are more likely to develop a positive self-image. Regularly offering praise for their efforts, celebrating their achievements, and providing constructive feedback can reinforce their sense of competence and worth. It is important that the praise is specific and sincere, focusing on the process rather than just the outcome.

Encouraging children to practice self-care is another effective strategy. Self-care activities, such as exercise, hobbies, relaxation techniques, and spending time with loved ones, can improve their overall well-being and reduce stress. When children feel good physically and emotionally, they are less likely to engage in negative self-talk.

It is also beneficial to teach children mindfulness and relaxation techniques. Practices such as mindfulness meditation can help children become more aware of their thoughts and feelings in the present moment, allowing them to identify and address negative self-talk as it arises. Relaxation techniques, such as deep breathing or progressive muscle relaxation, can help reduce anxiety and create a calmer state of mind, making it easier to challenge and change negative thoughts.

In some cases, professional support may be necessary. If negative self-talk is pervasive and significantly impacts a child's daily life and self-esteem, seeking help from a counselor or psychologist can be beneficial. These professionals can provide strategies and tools tailored to the child's specific needs and help them develop healthier thought patterns.

Ultimately, overcoming negative self-talk is an ongoing process that requires patience, consistency, and support. By helping children become aware of their internal dialogue, challenging negative thoughts, promoting positive affirmations, fostering a growth mindset, and providing a supportive environment, parents can equip their children with the tools they need to build a positive self-image and resilience. This journey not only enhances their self-esteem but also sets the foundation for a healthier and more fulfilling life.

# Chapter 2: Encouraging Creativity and Curiosity

## *2.1 The Importance of Creative Thinking*

Creative thinking is a crucial skill that enables individuals to approach problems and challenges in innovative and effective ways. For children, fostering creative thinking is essential for their cognitive development, academic success, and overall well-being. It allows them to express themselves, develop problem-solving skills, and build confidence in their abilities.

Creative thinking involves the ability to generate new ideas, see things from different perspectives, and make connections between seemingly unrelated concepts. It is not confined to artistic pursuits but extends to all areas of life, including science, mathematics, and social interactions. Encouraging creative thinking in children helps them develop a flexible mindset that is adaptable to various situations and challenges.

One of the most significant benefits of creative thinking is that it enhances problem-solving skills. Children who are encouraged to think creatively are better equipped to come up with multiple solutions to a problem, evaluate the pros and cons of each, and select the most effective one. This ability to think outside the box is invaluable in academic settings and later in life, where complex and multifaceted problems are common.

Creative thinking also promotes cognitive development by stimulating neural connections and enhancing brain plasticity. Engaging in creative activities such as drawing, storytelling, or playing with building blocks helps children develop fine motor skills, spatial awareness, and an understanding of cause and effect. These activities also encourage divergent thinking, which is the ability to generate many different ideas or solutions to a single problem.

Furthermore, creative thinking fosters emotional and social development. Through creative expression, children can explore their emotions, communicate their thoughts, and develop empathy. For instance, role-playing and storytelling allow children to put themselves in others' shoes, enhancing their understanding of different perspectives and emotions. This emotional intelligence is crucial for forming healthy relationships and navigating social interactions.

Encouraging creative thinking also builds confidence and resilience. When children are allowed to explore their ideas and take risks in a supportive environment, they learn that failure is a part of the creative process and an opportunity for growth. This resilience is essential for overcoming challenges and persisting in the face of setbacks. Additionally, successfully bringing their ideas to life boosts children's self-esteem and belief in their capabilities.

In the context of education, creative thinking is increasingly recognized as a critical skill for the 21st century. The rapidly changing job market demands individuals who can innovate, adapt, and think critically. By fostering creative thinking from an early age, we prepare children to thrive in diverse fields and contribute meaningfully to society. Schools that integrate creativity into their curricula report higher student engagement, improved academic performance, and enhanced problem-solving abilities.

Parents and educators play a vital role in nurturing creative thinking in children. Providing opportunities for open-ended play, encouraging curiosity, and creating a safe space for experimentation are key strategies. For example, offering a variety of materials such as art supplies, building blocks, and science kits can stimulate children's imagination and encourage them to explore different ways of using these materials. Additionally, allowing children the freedom to direct their play and make their own decisions fosters independence and creative thinking.

Reading and storytelling are also powerful tools for developing creativity. Books expose children to different worlds, characters, and scenarios, sparking their imagination and encouraging them to think creatively. Storytelling, whether through reading or creating their own stories, helps children understand narrative structure, develop language skills, and express their ideas.

Technology can also be harnessed to promote creative thinking. Educational apps and games that encourage problem-solving, design, and coding can be valuable resources. However, it is important to balance screen time with hands-on, unstructured play to ensure children develop a broad range of creative skills.

Encouraging creative thinking is not only about providing resources but also about fostering a mindset that values creativity. Praising children for their creative efforts, showing interest in their ideas, and modeling creative behavior are effective ways to cultivate a creative mindset. When children see adults engaging in creative activities and valuing innovation, they are more likely to adopt these attitudes themselves.

In conclusion, creative thinking is a vital skill that underpins many aspects of a child's development. It enhances problem-solving abilities, cognitive development, emotional intelligence, and resilience. By providing a supportive environment and valuing creativity, parents and educators can help children develop the creative thinking skills they need to succeed in a rapidly changing world.

## 2.2 Creating an Environment that Stimulates Curiosity

Curiosity is a powerful driver of learning and exploration. It fuels children's desire to understand the world around them, leading to discoveries and the development of critical thinking skills. Creating an environment that stimulates curiosity involves providing opportunities for exploration, encouraging questioning, and fostering a sense of wonder.

A key aspect of stimulating curiosity is providing a rich and varied environment. This means offering a wide range of materials and experiences that can pique children's interest and encourage them to explore. For young children, this might include sensory materials such as sand, water, and playdough, which allow them to experiment with textures, shapes, and physical properties. As children grow, providing access to books, art supplies, science kits, and building materials can further stimulate their curiosity and creativity.

Outdoor play is particularly effective in fostering curiosity. Nature provides endless opportunities for exploration and discovery. Simple activities such as observing insects, collecting leaves, or building structures with sticks and stones can captivate children's interest and encourage them to ask questions about the natural world. Outdoor environments also promote physical activity and a connection with nature, both of which are beneficial for overall well-being.

Creating a space that is visually stimulating and inviting can also spark curiosity. This could include displaying interesting objects, artwork, or educational materials at eye level where children can easily see and access them. Rotating these items regularly keeps the environment fresh and engaging. Additionally, setting up themed areas or stations, such as a reading nook, a science corner, or an art station, can encourage children to explore different activities and interests.

Encouraging curiosity involves more than just providing materials and space; it also requires fostering a supportive and open-minded attitude. Adults play a crucial role in modeling curiosity and a love of learning. When parents and educators express genuine interest in discovering new things, ask questions, and seek out answers, children are likely to mimic these behaviors. This creates a culture of curiosity where exploration and inquiry are valued.

One effective way to stimulate curiosity is to encourage children to ask questions and seek answers. Instead of providing immediate answers to their questions, adults can guide children in finding the answers themselves. This could involve looking up information together in books or online, conducting simple experiments, or observing and discussing the results. This process not only satisfies their curiosity but also teaches them valuable research and critical thinking skills.

Promoting a growth mindset is also important in stimulating curiosity. A growth mindset, the belief that abilities and intelligence can be developed through effort and learning, encourages children to embrace challenges and view failures as opportunities for growth. When children understand that making mistakes is a natural part of the learning process, they are more likely to take risks and explore new ideas without fear of failure.

Storytelling and reading are powerful tools for stimulating curiosity. Stories transport children to different worlds, introduce them to diverse characters and cultures, and spark their imagination. Reading books that explore various topics, from science and history to fantasy and adventure, can ignite a child's interest and inspire them to learn more about the subjects that captivate them.

Interactive and hands-on activities are particularly effective in stimulating curiosity. Activities that involve experimentation, problem-solving, and creative expression engage children's senses and minds. For example, cooking together can teach children about measurements, chemical reactions, and the origins of different foods. Building projects, such as constructing a model or designing a simple machine, can introduce concepts of engineering and physics.

In addition to structured activities, unstructured play is crucial for fostering curiosity. When children have the freedom to play without specific goals or instructions, they are more likely to explore, experiment, and discover new interests. Unstructured play allows children to follow their curiosity and creativity, leading to deeper and more meaningful learning experiences.

Creating an environment that stimulates curiosity also involves fostering a sense of wonder and appreciation for the world. Encouraging children to notice and reflect on the beauty and complexity of their surroundings can deepen their curiosity and desire to learn. This might include observing the changing seasons, marveling at the night sky, or discussing the intricate patterns found in nature.

In conclusion, creating an environment that stimulates curiosity involves providing a rich and varied setting, fostering a supportive and open-minded attitude, and encouraging exploration and questioning. By nurturing curiosity, parents and educators can help children develop a lifelong love of learning and a deeper understanding of the world around them.

## 2.3 *Encouraging Questions and Exploration*

Encouraging questions and exploration is fundamental to fostering a child's intellectual and emotional development. It involves creating a supportive environment where children feel safe and motivated to ask questions, seek answers, and engage in hands-on exploration. This process not only enhances their knowledge and skills but also cultivates a lifelong love of learning and discovery.

The first step in encouraging questions and exploration is to create a culture of curiosity and inquiry. This involves showing genuine interest in the world and modeling inquisitive behavior. When parents and educators express curiosity, ask questions, and actively seek out new information, they demonstrate that learning is a valuable and enjoyable pursuit. This behavior sets a positive example for children, encouraging them to adopt a similar approach.

A supportive environment is crucial for encouraging children to ask questions. Children need to feel that their questions are welcomed and valued. Adults should respond to questions with enthusiasm and patience, showing that they appreciate the child's curiosity. Even if the questions are challenging or seem trivial, taking the time to listen and engage with the child's inquiries fosters a sense of validation and encourages further questioning.

Responding to questions thoughtfully is important. Instead of providing immediate answers, adults can guide children in finding the answers themselves. This could involve discussing possible explanations, looking up information together, or conducting experiments. For example, if a child asks why the sky is blue, instead of simply explaining the science behind it, parents can explore the topic with the child through books, videos, or hands-on activities

that demonstrate how light interacts with the atmosphere. This approach not only satisfies the child's curiosity but also teaches them valuable research and critical thinking skills.

Encouraging open-ended questions is particularly beneficial. Open-ended questions, such as "What do you think will happen if...?" or "How might we solve this problem?", stimulate deeper thinking and creativity. They invite children to consider multiple possibilities and explore various perspectives, rather than seeking a single correct answer. This type of questioning promotes critical thinking and helps children develop the ability to analyze and synthesize information.

Providing opportunities for hands-on exploration is another effective way to encourage questions and discovery. Engaging children in activities that involve experimentation, problem-solving, and creative expression allows them to test their ideas and learn through experience. For instance, simple science experiments, building projects, or nature exploration can captivate children's interest and encourage them to ask questions about how things work and why they happen.

Unstructured play is also crucial for fostering exploration. When children have the freedom to play without specific goals or instructions, they are more likely to follow their curiosity and discover new interests. Unstructured play allows children to experiment with different materials, create their own rules, and explore their environment at their own pace. This type of play promotes independent thinking and innovation, as children learn to navigate and understand the world through their own experiences.

Books and storytelling are powerful tools for encouraging questions and exploration. Reading stories that introduce new concepts, cultures, and ideas can spark children's curiosity and inspire them to learn more. Interactive books that pose questions or present problems for the reader to solve are particularly effective. Storytelling sessions, where children are encouraged to create their own stories or contribute to a shared narrative, can also stimulate their imagination and prompt them to ask questions about the world and their experiences.

Incorporating technology thoughtfully can enhance exploration and learning. Educational apps and games that encourage problem-solving, design, and critical thinking can be valuable resources. Virtual field trips, interactive simulations, and online research tools can also provide children with opportunities to explore topics that interest them. However, it is important to balance screen time with hands-on, real-world activities to ensure a well-rounded approach to learning.

Creating a safe and supportive environment is essential for encouraging exploration. Children need to feel that they can take risks and make mistakes without fear of judgment or failure. When adults respond to children's efforts with encouragement and constructive feedback, they reinforce the idea that exploration and experimentation are valuable parts of the learning process. This support helps build children's confidence and resilience, encouraging them to persist in their inquiries and discoveries.

Additionally, fostering a growth mindset is important for encouraging questions and exploration. A growth mindset, the belief that abilities and intelligence can be developed through effort and learning, helps children see challenges and failures as opportunities for growth. When children understand that making mistakes is a natural part of learning, they are more likely to take risks, ask questions, and explore new ideas without fear of failure.

Encouraging collaboration and social learning can also enhance exploration. Group activities, discussions, and projects allow children to share their ideas, ask questions, and learn from each other. Collaborative learning environments promote communication, critical thinking, and problem-solving skills, as children work together to explore and understand new concepts.

In conclusion, encouraging questions and exploration involves creating a supportive environment, modeling inquisitive behavior, and providing opportunities for hands-on learning. By fostering a culture of curiosity and inquiry, parents and educators can help children develop the skills and mindset needed for lifelong learning and discovery.

## 2.4 Activities and Games to Boost Creativity

Boosting creativity in children is about providing them with opportunities to think outside the box, experiment, and express themselves in unique ways. Engaging them in a variety of activities and games can stimulate their imagination, encourage problem-solving, and develop their creative thinking skills. Here are some approaches to fostering creativity through different types of activities and games.

Artistic activities are a natural and effective way to boost creativity. Drawing, painting, and sculpting allow children to express their thoughts and emotions visually. These activities do not require strict guidelines or outcomes, which encourages children to explore different techniques and materials freely. For example, providing a range of art supplies, such as colored pencils, markers, watercolors, clay, and recycled materials, can inspire children to create original works of art. Encouraging them to draw or paint from their imagination, rather than copying, helps cultivate their unique creative voice.

Storytelling and writing activities are also excellent for fostering creativity. Encouraging children to write their own stories, whether through words or pictures, helps develop their narrative skills and imagination. Story cubes or prompts can be used to kickstart their creativity, offering a starting point for their tales. These cubes or cards can feature characters, settings, and plot twists that children can incorporate into their stories. Additionally, role-playing games, where children act out their stories or take on different characters, further stimulate their creative thinking and social skills.

Building and construction activities engage children in hands-on, spatial thinking and problem-solving. Toys like LEGO, blocks, and magnetic tiles provide endless possibilities for creating structures, vehicles, and imaginary worlds. These activities encourage children to think about design, balance, and engineering principles, all while engaging in play. Open-ended building challenges, such as constructing the tallest tower, creating a functional bridge, or designing a model of their dream house, can add an extra layer of excitement and creativity.

Music and movement activities are another effective way to boost creativity. Children can explore different instruments, sounds, and rhythms, experimenting with creating their own music. Simple instruments like drums, tambourines, and xylophones are accessible and fun for young children. Older children might enjoy learning to play a musical instrument, composing their own songs, or using digital tools to create music. Dance and movement activities, such as improvisational dance, can also stimulate creativity by encouraging children to express themselves through physical movement and rhythm.

Science experiments and exploration activities combine creativity with critical thinking and problem-solving. Simple experiments, such as making slime, baking soda and vinegar volcanoes, or growing crystals, allow children to hypothesize, observe, and draw conclusions. These activities often involve an element of unpredictability, which can spark curiosity and creative thinking. Nature-based activities, such as creating a nature journal, building a birdhouse, or exploring a local park, also encourage children to observe, question, and learn from their environment.

Games that promote creativity often involve open-ended play and imaginative scenarios. Board games like "Rory's Story Cubes," where players use dice with different images to create stories, or "Dixit," which involves interpreting abstract illustrations, are excellent for encouraging creative thinking and storytelling. These games not only foster imagination but also enhance language skills and social interaction. Similarly, card games like "Once Upon a Time," where players build a story collaboratively, encourage children to think on their feet and contribute creatively to a shared narrative.

Technology can also be a tool for boosting creativity when used thoughtfully. Digital art programs, coding games, and animation software offer children new mediums to express their creativity. Apps like "Toca Boca" and "Scratch" allow children to design characters, create interactive stories, and build their own games. These activities teach valuable digital literacy skills while providing a platform for creative expression.

Collaborative projects are another way to enhance creativity. Working together on group art projects, science experiments, or performances encourages children to share ideas, negotiate roles, and combine their talents. For example, creating a mural, putting on a play, or building a model city requires cooperation and communication, fostering both social and creative skills. Collaborative projects also teach children the value of diverse perspectives and the power of teamwork.

Encouraging outdoor and physical activities can also boost creativity. Outdoor play environments, such as playgrounds, gardens, and natural settings, provide rich opportunities for imaginative play and exploration. Activities like building forts, scavenger hunts, and nature art projects (such as making collages from leaves and flowers) engage children with their surroundings and stimulate creative thinking. Physical activities, such as obstacle courses or sports, can be adapted to include creative elements, like inventing new rules or games.

Finally, it is important to create an environment that supports and celebrates creativity. Displaying children's artwork, providing access to a variety of creative materials, and allowing time for unstructured play all contribute to a creative-friendly environment. Celebrating creative efforts, rather than just outcomes, reinforces the idea that creativity is valuable in itself. Offering positive feedback and encouragement helps build confidence and motivates children to continue exploring their creative potential.

In conclusion, boosting creativity in children involves providing a diverse range of activities and games that stimulate their imagination, problem-solving skills, and self-expression. From artistic and storytelling activities to building, music, science experiments, and collaborative projects, there are countless ways to encourage creativity. By creating a supportive and rich environment for creative exploration, parents and educators can help children develop into innovative and confident thinkers.

## 2.5 Balancing Structure and Freedom

Balancing structure and freedom in a child's life is crucial for their overall development. It involves providing a framework of routines and expectations while allowing ample opportunities for free exploration and self-directed play. This balance helps children develop discipline, responsibility, and self-regulation, along with creativity, independence, and problem-solving skills.

Structure provides children with a sense of security and predictability. Routines help children understand what to expect, which reduces anxiety and helps them feel in control. For example, having consistent bedtimes, mealtimes, and study times establishes a rhythm that supports physical and emotional well-being. Structured environments also teach children the importance of time management, responsibility, and following rules. Knowing that certain tasks, such as homework or chores, need to be completed at specific times instills discipline and a work ethic that benefits them throughout their lives.

However, too much structure can stifle creativity and inhibit a child's natural curiosity and desire to explore. Children need the freedom to engage in unstructured play, which is essential for their cognitive, social, and emotional development. Free play allows children to use their imagination, experiment with different roles, and solve problems independently. It is through unstructured play that children learn to make decisions, negotiate with peers, and develop resilience.

Finding the right balance between structure and freedom involves being flexible and responsive to a child's needs. It is important to provide guidelines and routines that offer stability while also allowing for flexibility when needed. For instance, while having a set bedtime is important, there can be occasional exceptions for special events or weekends. Similarly, while homework time might be scheduled, giving children some choice in the order they complete their tasks can help them feel more in control and engaged.

Incorporating free time into daily schedules is essential. This can be done by setting aside specific periods during the day where children can engage in activities of their choice without any imposed structure. During this time, they can explore their interests, be it through art, reading, playing outside, or engaging in imaginative play. Allowing children to follow their curiosity and pursue their passions fosters independence and intrinsic motivation.

Providing choices within a structured framework is another effective strategy. This approach gives children a sense of autonomy while still maintaining necessary boundaries. For example, during a scheduled reading time, children can choose which books they want to read. During mealtimes, offering a choice between two healthy options can make children feel empowered and involved in their routines. This blend of structure and choice helps children develop decision-making skills and a sense of responsibility.

Educational settings also benefit from balancing structure and freedom. Traditional schooling often emphasizes structured learning, but incorporating elements of self-directed learning can enhance student engagement and creativity. For instance, project-based learning allows students to explore topics that interest them within a structured framework. Teachers can set goals and provide resources, but students have the freedom to choose how they approach their projects and present their findings. This method not only promotes deeper understanding but also encourages students to take ownership of their learning.

Extracurricular activities can be structured in a way that balances guidance and freedom. For example, in a sports team, while there are rules and practices, allowing children to develop their own strategies or play different positions can foster creativity and teamwork. In art classes, while learning techniques and following certain guidelines is important, giving students freedom to create their own pieces can enhance their artistic expression and confidence.

Parental involvement plays a significant role in achieving this balance. Parents can set expectations and routines while also being attuned to their child's need for autonomy. It is important for parents to encourage exploration and support their child's interests, even if they differ from their own preferences. By listening to their children and providing a supportive environment, parents can help them develop both discipline and independence.

Technology, when used mindfully, can support the balance between structure and freedom. Educational apps and games can provide structured learning experiences, while creative tools and platforms allow children to explore and create independently. It is important to set guidelines for screen time and ensure that digital activities are balanced with physical play and face-to-face interactions.

Creating a physical environment that supports both structure and freedom is also beneficial. Designating specific areas for structured activities, such as a homework station or a reading nook, can help children focus and stay organized. At the same time, providing spaces for free play, such as a playroom or a backyard, encourages spontaneous and imaginative activities. Ensuring that children have access to a variety of materials and resources, from books and art supplies to outdoor toys and nature, can support their diverse interests and needs.

Incorporating downtime into schedules is crucial for maintaining a healthy balance. Children, like adults, need time to relax and unwind. Over-scheduling with structured activities can lead to stress and burnout. Ensuring that there are breaks throughout the day and unplanned weekends can provide children with the necessary rest and the freedom to engage in self-chosen activities.

Lastly, it is important to recognize that each child is unique, and what works for one may not work for another. Some children may thrive with more structure, while others may need more freedom to explore. Observing and understanding a child's temperament, preferences, and needs can help in tailoring the right balance for them. Communicating with children about their feelings and preferences can also provide valuable insights and help adjust routines and expectations accordingly.

Balancing structure and freedom is essential for fostering a child's development. While structure provides stability, security, and discipline, freedom allows for creativity, exploration, and independence. By creating an environment that respects both needs, parents and educators can support children in becoming well-rounded individuals who are capable of both following guidelines and thinking creatively. This balance not only prepares children for the demands of

the future but also nurtures their overall happiness and
well-being.

# Chapter 3: Enhancing Problem-Solving Skills

Problem-solving skills are essential for navigating life's challenges and achieving success in various domains, including academics, work, and personal relationships. Developing strong problem-solving skills equips children with the ability to analyze situations, identify solutions, and implement effective strategies to overcome obstacles. By fostering critical thinking, teaching problem-solving techniques, and encouraging independent thinking, parents and educators can help children become proficient problem solvers.

## 3.1 Developing Critical Thinking

Critical thinking is the foundation of effective problem-solving. It involves analyzing information, evaluating evidence, and making reasoned judgments. By developing critical thinking skills, children learn to approach problems systematically, consider multiple perspectives, and identify underlying assumptions.

Encouraging critical thinking begins with asking open-ended questions that prompt children to think deeply and reflect on their own reasoning. Instead of providing immediate answers, adults can guide children through a process of inquiry, helping them explore different possibilities and evaluate evidence. For example, when faced with a challenging problem, adults can ask questions such as "What do you already know about this problem?" or "What are some possible solutions, and what are their advantages and disadvantages?"

Engaging children in discussions that require them to defend their opinions or challenge others' viewpoints further develops critical thinking skills. Encouraging them to provide evidence to support their arguments and to consider counterarguments helps them become more discerning and analytical thinkers. Debates, group discussions, and Socratic questioning are effective strategies for promoting critical thinking in children.

Reading and analyzing complex texts also enhance critical thinking skills. Exposing children to diverse perspectives, conflicting opinions, and thought-provoking ideas encourages them to question assumptions and develop their own informed opinions. Encouraging children to identify the main ideas, evaluate evidence, and draw logical conclusions from texts helps them become more critical readers and thinkers.

Problem-solving activities that require logical reasoning and deductive thinking can also develop critical thinking skills. Puzzles, riddles, and logic games challenge children to analyze information, make connections, and apply deductive reasoning to arrive at solutions. These activities not only sharpen critical thinking skills but also foster persistence and resilience in the face of challenges.

## 3.2 Teaching Problem-Solving Techniques

Teaching specific problem-solving techniques equips children with practical strategies for approaching different types of problems. By introducing them to systematic problem-solving methods, children learn to break down complex problems into manageable steps and apply appropriate strategies to find solutions.

One effective problem-solving technique is the problem-solving cycle, which consists of several steps: understanding the problem, devising a plan, carrying out the plan, and evaluating the results. Teaching children to follow this structured approach helps them approach problems systematically and methodically. For example, when faced with a math problem, children can learn to read the problem carefully, identify relevant information, choose appropriate problem-solving strategies (such as drawing a diagram or making a list), and check their answers for accuracy.

Another valuable problem-solving technique is brainstorming, which encourages creativity and divergent thinking. Brainstorming involves generating multiple ideas or solutions without judgment or criticism. Teaching children to brainstorm effectively involves creating a supportive environment where all ideas are welcomed and valued. For example, when working on a group project, children can be encouraged to generate as many ideas as possible before evaluating and refining them.

Teaching children to use visual aids, such as diagrams, charts, and graphs, can also enhance problem-solving skills. Visual representations help children organize information, identify patterns, and visualize relationships between different elements of a problem. For example, when solving a word problem, children can draw a diagram to represent the information given and visually illustrate the relationships between the quantities involved.

Modeling problem-solving strategies and providing guided practice opportunities are essential for teaching problem-solving techniques. By demonstrating how to approach different types of problems and providing scaffolded support as children practice independently, adults help children develop confidence and proficiency in problem-solving. Gradually releasing responsibility to children as they become more competent allows them to apply problem-solving techniques autonomously.

## 3.3    Encouraging    Independent Thinking

Encouraging independent thinking empowers children to take ownership of their learning and develop confidence in their problem-solving abilities. By fostering autonomy and initiative, parents and educators help children become self-reliant and resourceful problem solvers.

Creating opportunities for independent exploration and experimentation is essential for encouraging independent thinking. Allowing children to pursue their interests and follow their curiosity without constant supervision or direction fosters independence and self-directed learning. For example, providing access to books, materials, and resources that align with children's interests encourages them to explore topics independently and develop their own ideas.

Encouraging children to take on challenges and persevere in the face of obstacles builds resilience and self-confidence. When children encounter difficulties, adults can offer guidance and support while encouraging them to find solutions independently. Praising their effort and persistence, rather than just their successes, reinforces the value of independent thinking and initiative.

Giving children opportunities to make decisions and take responsibility for their actions fosters independence and critical thinking skills. Allowing children to choose their own activities, set goals, and evaluate their progress encourages them to think critically about their choices and take ownership of their learning. Providing opportunities for leadership roles, such as leading a group discussion or organizing a project, further develops independence and self-confidence.

Encouraging children to question authority and think for themselves promotes independent thinking. Adults can model critical questioning and open-mindedness, demonstrating that it is acceptable to challenge assumptions and explore alternative perspectives. Engaging children in discussions about ethical dilemmas, controversial issues, and real-world problems encourages them to think critically and develop their own informed opinions.

Promoting a growth mindset is essential for encouraging independent thinking. A growth mindset, the belief that abilities and intelligence can be developed through effort and learning, fosters resilience and a willingness to take on challenges. When children understand that their abilities can grow with practice and perseverance, they are more likely to embrace challenges and persist in the face of setbacks.

Providing constructive feedback that focuses on effort and improvement, rather than just outcomes, reinforces the value of independent thinking and initiative. Encouraging children to reflect on their experiences, identify areas for improvement, and set goals for themselves promotes self-awareness and self-directed learning. By fostering a growth mindset and providing opportunities for reflection and self-assessment, parents and educators help children become independent thinkers and problem solvers.

In conclusion, enhancing problem-solving skills involves developing critical thinking, teaching problem-solving techniques, and encouraging independent thinking. By fostering critical thinking, children learn to analyze information, evaluate evidence, and make reasoned judgments. Teaching problem-solving techniques equips children with practical strategies for approaching different types of problems. Encouraging independent thinking empowers children to take ownership of their learning, develop confidence in their abilities, and become self-reliant problem solvers. Together, these approaches help children develop the skills and mindset needed to navigate life's challenges successfully.

## 3.4 Learning from Mistakes

Learning from mistakes is an essential aspect of problem-solving and personal growth. When children understand that mistakes are opportunities for learning and improvement, they become more resilient, adaptable, and confident problem solvers. By fostering a growth mindset and providing opportunities for reflection and growth, parents and educators can help children develop a positive attitude towards mistakes and setbacks.

Encouraging a growth mindset is crucial for fostering a healthy attitude towards mistakes. A growth mindset, as opposed to a fixed mindset, emphasizes the belief that abilities and intelligence can be developed through effort and learning. When children understand that making mistakes is a natural part of the learning process and that their abilities can improve with practice and perseverance, they are more likely to embrace challenges and persist in the face of setbacks.

Modeling a positive attitude towards mistakes is essential for promoting a growth mindset. Adults can demonstrate resilience and perseverance in the face of their own challenges and mistakes, showing children that setbacks are opportunities for learning and growth. Praise and recognition should focus on effort and improvement, rather than just outcomes, reinforcing the idea that mistakes are an essential part of the learning process.

Creating a safe and supportive environment is crucial for encouraging children to take risks and make mistakes. When children feel accepted and valued, they are more willing to try new things and push themselves outside their comfort zone. Adults should provide constructive feedback that focuses on the process rather than the result, helping children understand where they went wrong and how they can improve in the future.

Encouraging children to reflect on their mistakes and identify areas for improvement promotes self-awareness and personal growth. After making a mistake, adults can guide children through a process of reflection, asking questions such as "What happened?", "What could you have done differently?", and "What did you learn from this experience?" This process helps children recognize patterns in their thinking and behavior and develop strategies for avoiding similar mistakes in the future.

Encouraging children to view mistakes as opportunities for learning and growth rather than sources of shame or embarrassment is essential for building resilience and self-confidence. Adults can help children reframe their thinking by emphasizing the importance of perseverance and resilience in the face of setbacks. For example, instead of saying "You failed," adults can say "You haven't succeeded yet, but you're making progress." This subtle shift in language communicates the idea that mistakes are temporary setbacks that can be overcome with effort and perseverance.

Providing opportunities for children to experience failure in a safe and supportive environment helps desensitize them to the fear of making mistakes. For example, engaging children in challenging activities where failure is expected, such as puzzles or problem-solving games, helps them become more comfortable with the idea of making mistakes and learning from them. When children understand that failure is not the end of the road but rather a stepping stone to success, they become more resilient and adaptable problem solvers.

Encouraging children to take ownership of their mistakes and develop strategies for improvement promotes independence and self-directed learning. When children understand that they are responsible for their own learning and growth, they become more motivated to seek out solutions and overcome obstacles independently. Adults can guide children through a process of setting goals, monitoring their progress, and adjusting their strategies based on feedback, helping them develop the skills and mindset needed to succeed in the face of challenges.

In conclusion, learning from mistakes is an essential aspect of problem-solving and personal growth. By fostering a growth mindset, creating a safe and supportive environment, and encouraging reflection and self-improvement, parents and educators can help children develop a positive attitude towards mistakes and setbacks. When children understand that mistakes are opportunities for learning and growth rather than sources of shame or embarrassment, they become more resilient, adaptable, and confident problem solvers.

## 3.5 Interactive Problem-Solving Activities

Interactive problem-solving activities engage children in hands-on exploration and experimentation, helping them develop critical thinking, creativity, and collaboration skills. By providing opportunities for active learning and discovery, parents and educators can help children become proficient problem solvers who are capable of tackling real-world challenges.

Hands-on science experiments are an effective way to engage children in interactive problem-solving activities. These activities allow children to explore scientific concepts through observation, experimentation, and analysis. For example, conducting simple experiments such as making slime, creating chemical reactions with baking soda and vinegar, or building a bridge out of spaghetti noodles and marshmallows challenges children to apply scientific principles to solve problems and achieve desired outcomes.

Building and engineering activities encourage children to think critically and creatively as they design and construct structures, vehicles, and machines. Providing materials such as LEGO, blocks, magnetic tiles, and recycled materials allows children to experiment with different shapes, sizes, and configurations. By encouraging children to brainstorm ideas, plan their designs, and test their creations, adults foster problem-solving skills and spatial reasoning abilities.

Puzzle-solving games challenge children to use logic, spatial reasoning, and problem-solving skills to solve complex problems. Activities such as jigsaw puzzles, Sudoku, tangrams, and Rubik's cubes require children to analyze patterns, make connections, and think critically about their strategies. These games not only stimulate the brain but also promote perseverance and resilience as children work towards finding solutions.

Escape rooms and scavenger hunts provide interactive problem-solving experiences that challenge children to work together to solve puzzles and unravel mysteries. These activities require teamwork, communication, and critical thinking as children collaborate to decipher clues, solve riddles, and unlock hidden secrets. By engaging in these immersive experiences, children develop problem-solving skills in a fun and engaging way.

Role-playing games, such as detective mysteries or historical simulations, immerse children in interactive problem-solving scenarios where they must use their imagination and creativity to overcome obstacles and achieve their goals. These activities encourage children to think outside the box, explore different perspectives, and make decisions based on limited information. By assuming different roles and engaging in collaborative storytelling, children develop empathy, communication, and problem-solving skills.

Coding and robotics activities introduce children to computational thinking and problem-solving in a hands-on, interactive way. Programming games and apps teach children to break down complex problems into manageable steps, sequence instructions, and debug errors. Building and programming robots challenge children to apply mathematical concepts, logical reasoning, and algorithmic thinking to solve real-world problems.

Outdoor and nature-based activities provide opportunities for interactive problem-solving in natural settings. Activities such as scavenger hunts, treasure hunts, and nature exploration challenges children to use their observation skills, critical thinking, and creativity to solve puzzles and complete tasks. Outdoor games and sports also promote problem-solving skills as children navigate obstacles, make strategic decisions, and adapt to changing environments.

Interactive storytelling activities engage children in imaginative problem-solving adventures where they must make decisions and solve dilemmas to advance the plot. Activities such as choose-your-own-adventure stories, role-playing games, and collaborative storytelling exercises encourage children to think creatively, make choices, and explore different outcomes. By participating in these interactive narratives, children develop problem-solving skills while honing their storytelling abilities.

Virtual reality (VR) and augmented reality (AR) experiences provide immersive, interactive problem-solving opportunities that engage children in virtual worlds and simulations. VR escape rooms, puzzle games, and educational simulations challenge children to solve problems and complete tasks in a virtual environment. AR scavenger hunts and interactive storybooks bring digital content into the real world, blurring the lines between physical and virtual problem-solving experiences.

Interactive problem-solving activities engage children in hands-on exploration and experimentation, fostering critical thinking, creativity, and collaboration skills. By providing opportunities for active learning and discovery through science experiments, building activities, puzzle-solving games, escape rooms, role-playing games, coding and robotics, outdoor adventures, interactive storytelling, and virtual reality experiences, parents and educators can help children become proficient problem solvers who are capable of tackling real-world challenges with confidence and resilience.

# Chapter 4: Fostering Emotional Intelligence

Emotional intelligence (EI) plays a crucial role in children's overall well-being and success in life. It encompasses the ability to recognize, understand, and manage one's own emotions, as well as the capacity to empathize with others and navigate social relationships effectively. By fostering emotional intelligence, parents and educators can help children develop self-awareness, interpersonal skills, and resilience, which are essential for navigating the complexities of the modern world.

## 4.1 Understanding Emotional Intelligence

Emotional intelligence involves a range of skills and competencies that contribute to overall emotional well-being and social functioning. These skills include self-awareness, self-regulation, social awareness, empathy, and relationship management. Understanding emotional intelligence begins with recognizing the importance of emotions in shaping behavior, decisions, and interpersonal interactions.

Self-awareness is the foundation of emotional intelligence, as it involves recognizing and understanding one's own emotions, thoughts, and behaviors. Children who are self-aware are better able to identify their feelings, strengths, and weaknesses, which enables them to make more informed choices and set realistic goals. Parents and educators can promote self-awareness by encouraging children to reflect on their emotions and experiences, identify patterns in their behavior, and recognize how their thoughts and feelings influence their actions.

Self-regulation refers to the ability to manage and control one's emotions, impulses, and reactions effectively. Children who are able to self-regulate are better equipped to cope with stress, frustration, and adversity, leading to greater resilience and well-being. Teaching self-regulation involves helping children develop coping strategies, relaxation techniques, and problem-solving skills that enable them to manage their emotions and behaviors in challenging situations.

Social awareness involves understanding and empathizing with others' emotions, perspectives, and needs. Children who are socially aware are more attuned to the feelings and experiences of those around them, which fosters positive relationships and effective communication. Parents and educators can promote social awareness by encouraging children to practice active listening, perspective-taking, and empathy, as well as by exposing them to diverse perspectives and experiences.

Empathy is the ability to understand and share the feelings of others, which is essential for building strong interpersonal relationships and fostering cooperation and compassion. Children who are empathetic are more likely to be kind, supportive, and respectful towards others, leading to greater social connectedness and well-being. Teaching empathy involves helping children recognize and validate others' emotions, perspective-take, and demonstrate caring and concern for others' well-being.

Relationship management involves effectively navigating social interactions, resolving conflicts, and building positive relationships with others. Children who are skilled in relationship management are better able to communicate assertively, collaborate with others, and negotiate differences, leading to healthier and more satisfying relationships. Parents and educators can promote relationship management by teaching children conflict resolution skills, assertive communication techniques, and strategies for building trust and rapport with others.

## 4.2   Identifying   and   Managing Emotions

Identifying and managing emotions is a fundamental aspect of emotional intelligence that begins in early childhood and continues throughout life. Children who are able to recognize and regulate their emotions are better equipped to cope with stress, form positive relationships, and achieve their goals. Parents and educators play a crucial role in helping children develop these essential skills.

Helping children identify and label their emotions is the first step in emotional self-awareness. Parents and educators can teach children to recognize and name different emotions by providing them with a vocabulary of feeling words and encouraging them to express their emotions verbally. Reading books, watching videos, and engaging in discussions about emotions can also help children learn to identify and understand their feelings.

Teaching children to recognize the physical sensations associated with different emotions can also enhance emotional self-awareness. Encouraging children to pay attention to their bodily reactions, such as changes in heart rate, breathing, and muscle tension, helps them connect their physical sensations to their emotional experiences. Mindfulness practices, such as deep breathing exercises and body scans, can help children develop greater awareness of their bodily sensations and emotions.

Once children are able to identify their emotions, teaching them strategies for managing their emotions effectively is essential. Parents and educators can help children develop a toolbox of coping strategies, such as deep breathing, progressive muscle relaxation, visualization, and positive self-talk, that they can use to regulate their emotions in challenging situations. Encouraging children to practice these strategies regularly helps them build resilience and self-confidence.

Teaching children to recognize and challenge unhelpful thought patterns, such as negative self-talk and catastrophizing, is also important for emotional self-regulation. Helping children reframe their thoughts in a more positive and realistic way empowers them to change how they feel and behave in response to challenging situations. Cognitive-behavioral techniques, such as cognitive restructuring and thought challenging, can help children develop more adaptive ways of thinking and responding to stress.

## 4.3 Teaching Empathy and Compassion

Empathy and compassion are essential components of emotional intelligence that enable children to understand and connect with others' emotions, experiences, and perspectives. By teaching empathy and compassion, parents and educators can help children develop strong interpersonal relationships, promote kindness and empathy, and foster a sense of social responsibility.

Modeling empathy and compassion is the first step in teaching these important values to children. Parents and educators can demonstrate empathy and compassion in their own interactions with others by listening attentively, expressing understanding and validation, and offering support and encouragement. By modeling caring and empathetic behavior, adults provide children with a powerful example to emulate in their own interactions with others.

Encouraging perspective-taking is another effective way to teach empathy and compassion. Perspective-taking involves imagining oneself in another person's shoes and understanding their thoughts, feelings, and experiences from their point of view. Parents and educators can help children develop perspective-taking skills by encouraging them to consider how others might feel in different situations and to reflect on the impact of their words and actions on others.

Promoting kindness and empathy through acts of service and community involvement helps children develop a sense of social responsibility and compassion for others. Engaging children in volunteer activities, acts of kindness, and community service projects provides them with opportunities to practice empathy and compassion in real-world contexts. By giving back to others and making a positive difference in their communities, children learn the importance of empathy, compassion, and social justice.

Encouraging cooperative play and teamwork is another effective way to teach empathy and compassion. Collaborative activities, such as group projects, team sports, and cooperative games, provide children with opportunities to work together towards a common goal, practice empathy, and develop interpersonal skills. By promoting cooperation, communication, and mutual respect, adults help children learn to navigate social relationships and build strong interpersonal connections.

## 4.4 Strategies for Emotional Regulation

Emotional regulation refers to the ability to manage and control one's emotions effectively, which is essential for overall well-being and success in life. Children who are able to regulate their emotions are better equipped to cope with stress, build positive relationships, and achieve their goals. By teaching children strategies for emotional regulation, parents and educators can help them develop resilience, self-confidence, and emotional well-being.

One effective strategy for emotional regulation is deep breathing exercises. Deep breathing helps activate the body's relaxation response, which counteracts the stress response and promotes a sense of calm and relaxation. Teaching children simple deep breathing techniques, such as belly breathing or square breathing, empowers them to regulate their emotions and calm themselves down when feeling stressed or overwhelmed.

Progressive muscle relaxation is another effective technique for promoting emotional regulation. Progressive muscle relaxation involves tensing and relaxing different muscle groups in the body,

 which helps release physical tension and reduce feelings of anxiety and stress. Teaching children progressive muscle relaxation exercises, such as tensing and releasing their fists, arms, shoulders, and legs, helps them become more aware of their physical sensations and learn to relax their bodies in response to stress.

Visualization and guided imagery are powerful techniques for promoting emotional regulation and relaxation. Visualization involves imagining oneself in a peaceful and calming place, such as a beach or a forest, and focusing on the sights, sounds, and sensations of that environment. Guided imagery involves listening to a recorded script or audio track that guides children through a visualization exercise, helping them relax and unwind. Teaching children to use visualization and guided imagery as tools for emotional regulation empowers them to create a sense of inner peace and calmness, even in the midst of challenging situations.

Encouraging positive self-talk is another effective strategy for promoting emotional regulation. Positive self-talk involves using encouraging and supportive language to challenge negative thoughts and beliefs, promote self-confidence, and boost resilience. Teaching children to reframe negative self-talk into positive affirmations, such as "I can do this" or "I am capable and strong," helps them develop a more optimistic and resilient mindset. By promoting positive self-talk, parents and educators help children cultivate a greater sense of self-worth and confidence in their abilities.

## 4.5 Role-Playing and Real-Life Scenarios

Role-playing and real-life scenarios provide opportunities for children to practice emotional regulation skills in a safe and supportive environment. By engaging in role-playing activities and acting out real-life scenarios, children learn to recognize and respond to different emotions, develop empathy and perspective-taking skills, and practice effective communication and problem-solving strategies.

Role-playing allows children to step into different roles and explore different perspectives, which promotes empathy and understanding. By pretending to be someone else, children learn to see things from another person's point of view and empathize with their thoughts, feelings, and experiences. Role-playing also helps children develop interpersonal skills, such as active listening, assertive communication, and conflict resolution, as they navigate social interactions and negotiate with others.

Engaging children in role-playing activities that involve emotional scenarios, such as conflicts with friends, disagreements with siblings, or encounters with bullies, helps them practice emotional regulation skills in realistic contexts. By acting out these scenarios and exploring different responses, children learn to recognize their own emotions, manage their reactions, and communicate effectively with others. Role-playing also provides opportunities for adults to provide feedback and guidance, helping children develop more adaptive and effective coping strategies.

Real-life scenarios provide children with opportunities to apply their emotional regulation skills in authentic contexts. By discussing real-life situations that children may encounter, such as getting lost in a store, receiving criticism from a teacher, or feeling left out by friends, parents and educators help children anticipate and prepare for challenging situations. Encouraging children to brainstorm strategies for managing their emotions and solving problems in these situations empowers them to respond effectively when faced with similar challenges in the future.

Using storytelling and literature as a tool for exploring emotional scenarios is another effective strategy for promoting emotional regulation. Reading books, watching movies, or listening to stories that feature characters experiencing a range of emotions allows children to empathize with the characters' feelings and experiences and learn from their struggles and successes. By discussing the characters' emotions and behaviors, parents and educators help children develop a deeper understanding of their own emotions and learn valuable lessons about emotional regulation and resilience.

Fostering emotional intelligence involves helping children understand and manage their emotions, empathize with others, and navigate social relationships effectively. By teaching children to recognize and regulate their emotions, promoting empathy and compassion, and providing strategies for emotional regulation, parents and educators help children develop the skills and resilience needed to thrive in today's complex world. Role-playing and real-life scenarios provide valuable opportunities for children to practice emotional regulation skills in realistic contexts, develop empathy and perspective-taking skills, and learn effective communication and problem-solving strategies. By fostering emotional intelligence, adults empower children to become confident, compassionate, and resilient individuals who are capable of building positive relationships and achieving their goals.

# Chapter 5: Building a Strong Parent-Child Relationship

A strong parent-child relationship is the bedrock of a child's emotional and psychological development. It lays the foundation for trust, security, and emotional well-being, and it shapes the child's sense of self, their social interactions, and their future relationships. By investing time and effort into nurturing a strong bond with their children, parents can create a supportive and loving environment where children feel valued, understood, and empowered to thrive.

## 5.1 *The Foundations of a Loving Relationship*

The foundations of a loving parent-child relationship are built on a combination of unconditional love, acceptance, and consistency. Unconditional love forms the basis of the parent-child bond, providing children with a sense of security and belonging that is essential for their emotional development. When children feel loved and accepted for who they are, they develop a strong sense of self-worth and confidence that enables them to explore the world and form healthy relationships.

Acceptance is another key component of a loving relationship, as it involves embracing and celebrating each child's unique qualities, strengths, and quirks. When parents accept their children unconditionally, regardless of their achievements or shortcomings, they communicate that their love is not contingent on performance or behavior. This creates a safe and nurturing environment where children feel free to express themselves authentically and develop a positive self-image.

Consistency in parenting is essential for building trust and security in the parent-child relationship. When parents are reliable, predictable, and consistent in their responses to their children's needs and behaviors, children learn to trust that their parents will be there for them and provide the support and guidance they need. Consistency also helps establish clear boundaries and expectations, which are important for children's sense of safety and structure.

## 5.2 Effective Communication Techniques

Effective communication is the cornerstone of a strong parent-child relationship, as it fosters understanding, trust, and connection between parents and children. By practicing active listening, empathy, and validation, parents can create an open and supportive environment where children feel heard, understood, and valued.

Active listening involves giving children your full attention and focusing on what they are saying without judgment or interruption. When parents listen attentively to their children's thoughts, feelings, and experiences, they communicate that their opinions and perspectives are important and worthy of consideration. This helps children feel valued and respected, which strengthens the parent-child bond.

Empathy is the ability to understand and share another person's feelings, which is essential for effective communication and emotional connection. When parents demonstrate empathy towards their children's experiences, they validate their feelings and help them feel understood and supported. Empathetic responses, such as "I can see that you're feeling sad" or "That sounds really frustrating," communicate that parents are attuned to their children's emotions and are there to offer comfort and support.

Validation involves acknowledging and accepting children's thoughts, feelings, and experiences without judgment or criticism. When parents validate their children's emotions, even if they don't agree with them, they communicate that their feelings are valid and worthy of respect. This helps children feel accepted and understood, which strengthens their sense of self-worth and confidence.

## 5.3 Spending Quality Time Together

Spending quality time together is essential for building a strong parent-child relationship and fostering emotional connection and bonding. Quality time involves engaging in activities that promote meaningful interaction, communication, and shared experiences between parents and children.

One-on-one time is important for nurturing individual relationships between parents and each of their children. By setting aside dedicated time to spend with each child, parents can create opportunities for focused attention, conversation, and bonding. This helps children feel valued and cherished as individuals, which strengthens their sense of security and belonging within the family.

Family rituals and traditions are another effective way to spend quality time together and create lasting memories. Whether it's sharing meals, playing games, or participating in holiday traditions, family rituals provide opportunities for bonding, laughter, and connection. By establishing and maintaining family rituals, parents create a sense of continuity and stability that strengthens the family bond.

Shared interests and hobbies provide opportunities for parents and children to connect over common passions and activities. Whether it's sports, music, art, or cooking, engaging in shared activities allows parents and children to bond over shared experiences and create lasting memories together. By supporting and participating in their children's interests, parents show that they value their children's passions and are invested in their happiness and well-being.

Outdoor adventures and nature outings provide opportunities for families to unplug, connect with nature, and enjoy each other's company away from the distractions of everyday life. Whether it's hiking, camping, or simply exploring the outdoors, spending time in nature allows families to bond over shared experiences and create memories that will last a lifetime. Outdoor activities also promote physical health and well-being, which further strengthens the parent-child relationship.

Building a strong parent-child relationship requires a combination of unconditional love, acceptance, effective communication, and quality time together. By creating a supportive and nurturing environment where children feel valued, understood, and empowered to thrive, parents lay the foundation for their children's emotional and psychological development. By investing time and effort into nurturing a strong bond with their children, parents can create a lasting legacy of love, connection, and resilience that will benefit their children for a lifetime.

## 5.4 Handling Conflicts and Disagreements

Conflicts and disagreements are a natural part of any relationship, including the parent-child relationship. How these conflicts are handled can significantly impact the strength and health of the relationship. By employing effective conflict resolution strategies, parents can teach their children valuable skills for managing conflict in their own lives and strengthen the bond between them.

### Understanding Conflict

Conflict arises when there are differences in opinions, values, or needs between individuals. In the parent-child relationship, conflicts can occur over a variety of issues, such as rules and boundaries, chores, homework, or personal preferences. It's important for both parents and children to recognize that conflicts are normal and inevitable, and that they can be opportunities for growth and learning when handled constructively.

## Active Listening

One of the most important skills in resolving conflicts is active listening. Active listening involves giving the other person your full attention, suspending judgment, and seeking to understand their perspective. When conflicts arise between parents and children, it's essential for both parties to listen to each other's concerns and feelings without interrupting or becoming defensive.

## Expressing Feelings Constructively

Both parents and children should feel free to express their feelings openly and honestly during conflicts, but it's important to do so constructively. This means avoiding blaming, name-calling, or using hurtful language. Instead, individuals should focus on expressing their own feelings and needs using "I" statements, such as "I feel frustrated when..." or "I need..." This helps keep the conversation focused on finding solutions rather than escalating into a heated argument.

## Finding Common Ground

During conflicts, it's important for both parties to look for areas of agreement or compromise. Finding common ground can help de-escalate tensions and move the conversation towards a resolution. Parents and children should work together to brainstorm potential solutions that address both parties' needs and concerns, and be willing to negotiate and make concessions when necessary.

## Setting Boundaries and Consequences

In some cases, conflicts may arise over issues where boundaries have been crossed or rules have been broken. In these situations, it's important for parents to communicate clear expectations and consequences for behavior. Setting boundaries helps establish a sense of structure and predictability in the parent-child relationship, and provides a framework for resolving conflicts when they arise.

## Apologizing and Forgiving

When conflicts occur, it's important for both parties to take responsibility for their actions and apologize if necessary. Apologizing demonstrates humility and respect, and helps repair any damage done to the relationship. Likewise, forgiveness is essential for moving past conflicts and rebuilding trust. Parents and children should be willing to forgive each other and move forward with a renewed commitment to understanding and cooperation.

## Seeking Professional Help if Needed

In some cases, conflicts between parents and children may be more complex or difficult to resolve on their own. In these situations, seeking the help of a qualified therapist or counselor can be beneficial. A therapist can provide a neutral and supportive environment where both parties can express their feelings and work towards finding solutions. Family therapy can also help improve communication and strengthen the parent-child relationship.

## 5.5 The Role of Trust and Respect

Trust and respect are fundamental aspects of any healthy relationship, including the parent-child relationship. When parents and children trust and respect each other, they are able to communicate openly and honestly, resolve conflicts constructively, and support each other's growth and development.

### *Building Trust*

Trust is built over time through consistent actions and behaviors that demonstrate reliability, honesty, and integrity. Parents can build trust with their children by following through on their promises, being honest and transparent in their communication, and respecting their children's boundaries and privacy. Trust is essential for creating a secure and nurturing environment where children feel safe to express themselves and seek support from their parents.

## Respecting Boundaries

Respecting boundaries is an important aspect of building trust and respect in the parent-child relationship. Boundaries are guidelines that define the limits of acceptable behavior and personal space. Parents should respect their children's boundaries by honoring their privacy, listening to their concerns, and avoiding intrusive or controlling behavior. Respecting boundaries helps children feel valued and respected as individuals, and fosters a sense of autonomy and independence.

## Open Communication

Open communication is essential for building trust and respect between parents and children. Parents should create a supportive and non-judgmental environment where children feel comfortable expressing their thoughts, feelings, and concerns. Encouraging open communication helps parents stay connected with their children's lives, understand their perspectives, and address any issues or challenges they may be facing. Regular communication builds trust and strengthens the parent-child bond.

## Honoring Differences

Respecting each other's differences is an important aspect of building trust and respect in the parent-child relationship. Every child is unique and has their own personality, interests, and preferences. Parents should honor and celebrate their children's individuality, even if it differs from their own expectations or desires. Accepting and embracing differences fosters a sense of mutual respect and appreciation, and strengthens the parent-child bond.

## *Modeling Respectful Behavior*

Parents play a crucial role in modeling respectful behavior for their children. Children learn how to respect others by observing how their parents treat them and others. Parents should strive to demonstrate kindness, empathy, and consideration in their interactions with their children, as well as with others in their lives. Modeling respectful behavior helps children learn how to treat others with dignity and respect, and reinforces the importance of trust and mutual understanding in relationships.

## *Resolving Conflicts Constructively*

Resolving conflicts constructively is another important aspect of building trust and respect in the parent-child relationship. When conflicts arise, parents and children should strive to communicate openly and honestly, listen to each other's perspectives, and work together to find mutually acceptable solutions. Resolving conflicts in a respectful and collaborative manner strengthens the parent-child bond and fosters a sense of trust and understanding between both parties.

In conclusion, trust and respect are essential components of a strong and healthy parent-child relationship. By building trust through consistent actions and behaviors, respecting each other's boundaries and differences, fostering open communication, modeling respectful behavior, and resolving conflicts constructively, parents can create a supportive and nurturing environment where children feel valued, understood, and empowered to thrive. Trust and respect form the foundation of a strong parent-child bond, and are essential for promoting positive communication, resolving conflicts, and supporting each other's growth and development.

# Chapter 6: Integrating Recreative Parenting in Daily Life

Integrating recreative parenting into daily life involves incorporating strategies and principles that promote children's development and well-being into everyday routines and activities. By establishing routines, balancing work and family life, implementing practical tips, overcoming challenges, and celebrating milestones, parents can create a nurturing and supportive environment where children can thrive.

## 6.1 Establishing Routine and Consistency

Routine and consistency are essential for creating a sense of stability and predictability in children's lives. Establishing daily routines for activities such as mealtimes, bedtime, and homework can help children feel secure and confident, as they know what to expect and what is expected of them. Consistency in parenting practices, such as setting and enforcing rules and boundaries, also helps children understand what is acceptable behavior and fosters a sense of trust and security in the parent-child relationship.

## 6.2 Balancing Work, Life, and Parenting

Balancing work, life, and parenting can be challenging, but it is essential for maintaining overall well-being and harmony in the family. Parents can prioritize their time and energy by setting boundaries, delegating tasks, and practicing self-care. Finding ways to involve children in daily activities, such as meal preparation or household chores, can also help strengthen the parent-child bond and teach valuable life skills.

## 6.3 Practical Tips for Busy Parents

Busy parents can incorporate recreative parenting strategies into their daily lives by finding creative ways to engage with their children, even amidst busy schedules. Simple activities such as reading together before bedtime, having family meals, or going for walks in nature can provide opportunities for bonding and connection. Additionally, using technology mindfully, such as scheduling screen-free times or using educational apps and games, can help parents balance the benefits and drawbacks of digital media.

## 6.4 Overcoming Common Parenting Challenges

Parenting comes with its own set of challenges, but by approaching them with a positive mindset and seeking support when needed, parents can overcome obstacles and grow stronger as a family. Common challenges such as managing behavior, dealing with sibling rivalry, or navigating transitions can be addressed through open communication, problem-solving, and seeking guidance from trusted sources such as parenting books, support groups, or professional counselors.

## 6.5 Celebrating Progress and Milestones

Celebrating progress and milestones, no matter how small, is important for reinforcing positive behavior and building children's self-esteem. Parents can acknowledge and praise their children's efforts and achievements, whether it's mastering a new skill, showing kindness towards others, or overcoming a challenge. By recognizing and celebrating these moments, parents can foster a sense of pride and accomplishment in their children, which motivates them to continue growing and learning.

In conclusion, integrating recreative parenting into daily life involves incorporating strategies and principles that promote children's development and well-being into everyday routines and activities. By establishing routines, balancing work and family life, implementing practical tips, overcoming challenges, and celebrating milestones, parents can create a nurturing and supportive environment where children can thrive. Through mindful parenting practices and a commitment to fostering positive relationships, parents can create lasting memories and instill values that will benefit their children throughout their lives.

# Conclusion

In the journey of parenting, adopting recreative parenting strategies offers a holistic approach to nurturing children's growth and development. As we conclude this exploration, let's recap the key strategies, delve into the long-term benefits of recreative parenting, and discuss how to continue this journey in the future.

## *Recap of Key Strategies*

Throughout this book, we've explored various strategies to foster confident, creative, and emotionally intelligent children:

- Building Self-Worth and Self-Acceptance: By nurturing a deep sense of self-worth and acceptance, parents lay the foundation for their children's confidence and resilience.

- Encouraging Creativity and Curiosity: Stimulating children's creativity and curiosity not only fuels their imagination but also enhances their problem-solving skills and adaptability.

- Developing Emotional Intelligence: Teaching children to recognize, understand, and manage their emotions fosters empathy, communication, and healthy relationships.

- **Building a Strong Parent-Child Relationship:** Establishing trust, communication, and mutual respect forms the basis of a supportive and nurturing parent-child bond.

- Integrating Recreative Parenting in Daily Life: Balancing routines, work, and practical tips allows parents to incorporate recreative parenting strategies into their busy lives seamlessly.

## Long-Term Benefits of Recreative Parenting

The long-term benefits of adopting recreative parenting strategies extend far beyond childhood:

- Resilient and Confident Adults: Children raised with a strong sense of self-worth, creativity, and emotional intelligence are better equipped to navigate life's challenges and thrive in adulthood.

- Healthy Relationships: A strong parent-child relationship built on trust, communication, and respect lays the groundwork for healthy relationships with others throughout life.

- Lifelong Learning: Encouraging curiosity, creativity, and problem-solving skills fosters a love for learning that extends beyond formal education and enriches every aspect of life.

- Emotional Well-being: Developing emotional intelligence equips children with the tools to navigate complex emotions, form meaningful connections, and lead fulfilling lives.

## *Continuing the Journey*

As we conclude this journey, it's important to remember that parenting is an ongoing process filled with learning and growth. Here are some ways to continue the journey of recreative parenting:

- Reflect and Adapt: Take time to reflect on your parenting journey, celebrate successes, and identify areas for growth. Be open to adapting your strategies as your child's needs and interests evolve.

- Stay Connected: Seek support from other parents, join parenting groups or communities, and stay connected with resources such as books, articles, and workshops to continue learning and growing as a parent.

- Prioritize Self-Care: Remember to prioritize your own well-being as a parent. Taking care of yourself physically, emotionally, and mentally allows you to show up fully for your children and model healthy behaviors.

- Celebrate Every Moment: Cherish the precious moments you share with your children and celebrate their growth and accomplishments, no matter how small. Every milestone is a testament to your love, dedication, and commitment as a parent.

Adopting recreative parenting strategies empowers parents to nurture confident, creative, and emotionally intelligent children who are prepared to thrive in an ever-changing world. By fostering a supportive and nurturing environment, building strong parent-child relationships, and prioritizing holistic development, parents can set their children on a path towards lifelong success and fulfillment. As we continue this journey of parenting, let us embrace the joys, challenges, and opportunities that lie ahead, knowing that the love and guidance we provide today will shape the future of our children tomorrow.

www.ingramcontent.com/pod-product-compliance
Lightning Source LLC
Chambersburg PA
CBHW051818250726
48659CB00005B/1545